Akira to Zoltán

Twenty-Six Men Who Changed the World

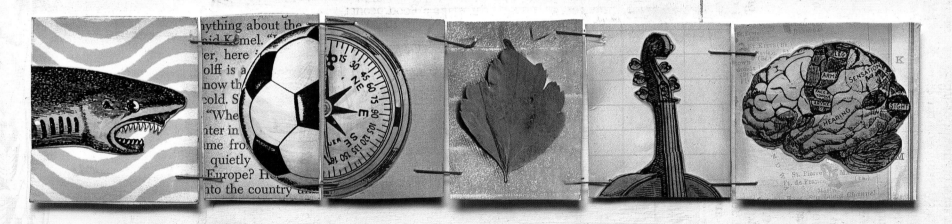

Cynthia Chin-Lee   Illustrated by Megan Halsey and Sean Addy

ini Charlesbridge

To Peter Ching when he was a little boy—C. C.

To the men who have changed MY world: Marty, Herbert, Jeff,
Bill and Brother Bill, Steve, Sean, and especially Dad—M. H.

To Pop and Dad Addy, Granpa R. and Dad Norberg, and all the MEN in the family.
Thanks for letting me in.—S. A.

Text copyright © 2006 by Cynthia Chin-Lee
Illustrations copyright © 2006 by Megan Halsey and Sean Addy

Published by Charlesbridge
85 Main Street
Watertown, MA 02472
(617) 926-0329
www.charlesbridge.com

Library of Congress Cataloging-in-Publication Data
Chin-Lee, Cynthia.
    Akira to Zoltán : twenty-six men who changed the world / Cynthia Chin-Lee;
illustrated by Megan Halsey and Sean Addy.
        p. cm.
    ISBN-13: 978-1-57091-579-6; ISBN-10: 1-57091-579-2 (reinforced for library use)
1. Biography—Juvenile literature. 2. Heroes—Biography—Juvenile
literature. 3. Men—Biography—Juvenile literature. I. Halsey, Megan.
II. Addy, Sean. III. Title.
CT107.C435 006
920.7109'04—dc22   2005027446

Printed in Korea
(hc) 10 9 8 7 6 5 4 3 2 1

Illustrations done in mixed media
Display type set in Amigo and text type set in New Baskerville and Greco Bold
Color separations by Chroma Graphics, Singapore
Printed and bound by Sung In Printing, South Korea
Production supervision by Brian G. Walker
Designed by Diane Earley and Susan Mallory Sherman

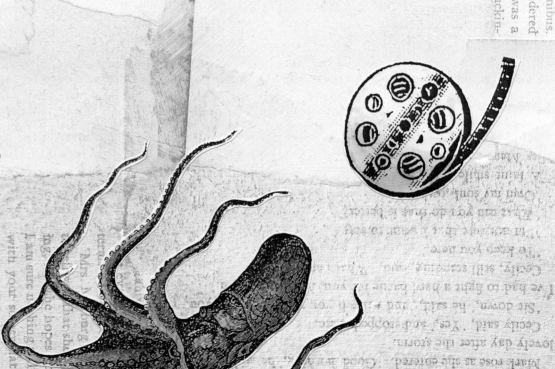

A is for Akira, film director and

screenwriter. As a young man Akira Kurosawa wanted to study painting, but he failed the art-school exam. A lifelong movie fan, he happened to read an ad for an assistant director at a studio. He applied for the job and beat out hundreds to win the position.

Akira finally found his calling; filmmaking allowed him to use his love of painting, literature, theater, and music. By his early thirties he had written and directed his first film, *Sugata Sanshiro,* which became a hit. Despite this early success, Akira faced criticism from studio management and reviewers for his experimental style. Still he persisted and directed films such as *Rashomon, Ikiru* (To Live), and *The Seven Samurai,* winning international acclaim and influencing Western cinema.

Always socially conscious, Akira made movies with such universal themes as the senselessness of war, the value of nature, and the meaning of life. Akira directed over 30 films, many of which he also wrote. During his career he won top honors at the Venice International Film Festival and several Academy Awards, including an Honorary Academy Award for lifetime achievement.

"For me, the only question is how can man find happiness with others."

AKIRA KUROSAWA (1910–1998)

B is for Badshah, "King of

the Khans." Born Abdul Ghaffar Khan, he was given the title Badshah, which means "king." Badshah Khan was the youngest child of a Pashtun village chief, or khan. The Pashtun people lived in what was once India's northwest territories, now part of Pakistan. Growing up on his family's farm, Badshah was an intense child whose two best friends were simple sweepers.

Although he was a devout Muslim, Badshah attended a high school run by British missionaries. After graduation he was offered a commission in the British Guides, an elite army unit, but after seeing a Pashtun guide insulted by a British soldier, he refused his commission. Restless to serve others, he started a series of Muslim schools.

Later inspired by Gandhi, Badshah recruited Pashtun men to join his nonviolent movement for ousting the British from India. Despite being imprisoned many times, he led the world's largest nonviolent force, 100,000 Khudai Khidmatgars (servants of God), for social reform in Pashtun lands.

"No true effort is in vain. Look at the fields over there. The grain sown therein has to remain in the earth for a certain time, then it sprouts, and in due time yields hundreds of its kind. The same is the case with every effort in a good cause."

BADSHAH ABDUL GHAFFAR KHAN (1890–1988)

C is for Cesar, co-founder of the United Farm Workers (UFW). Cesar Estrada Chavez was only 10 years old when his family lost their farm. They moved from Arizona to California and became migrant workers, traveling from farm to farm to pick crops. Cesar attended over 30 elementary schools during this time. He left school after eighth grade to become a farm worker.

Many years later Cesar worked for the Community Service Organization, a group that served the poor. But remembering the suffering of farm workers, he quit his job to help them instead.

In 1962 Cesar and co-founder Dolores Huerta created the National Farm Workers Association, which later became the UFW. They organized a boycott against grape growers. Cesar accepted a small salary and fasted for weeks to draw attention to the unhealthy conditions and low pay of workers. By 1970 the boycott forced growers to provide workers with higher pay, family health coverage, and protection from pesticides.

"Nonviolence is hard work. It is the willingness to sacrifice. It is the patience to win."

CESAR ESTRADA CHAVEZ (1927–1993)

D is for Diego,

painter of the people. Born in the mountains of Mexico, Diego María Rivera fell sick as a child, so his parents sent him to live with an Indian healer, Antonia. When he was strong, he returned to his parents, who gave him colored chalk as a homecoming present. Because Diego loved drawing, his father built him a room covered in blackboards so he could draw all over the walls. Yearning to study art, Diego left school to attend art classes. He painted what he saw around him, not just happy scenes like fiestas, but also scary ones like soldiers shooting striking workers.

After studying art in Europe, Diego returned to Mexico to paint the stories of his country—bold, colorful murals that honored the common people. He wanted art for all, not just the rich, and his murals decorated public areas where everyone could see them: in schools, plazas, and public buildings.

"An artist is above all a human being, profoundly human to the core. If the artist can't feel everything that humanity feels, if the artist isn't capable of loving until he forgets himself and sacrifices himself if necessary, if he won't put down his magic brush and head the fight against the oppressor, then he isn't a great artist."

DIEGO MARÍA RIVERA (1886–1957)

7

E is for Ellison, American

astronaut. Ellison Shoji Onizuka was born in Kona, Hawaii, and like many children, he dreamed of being an astronaut. As a young child he enjoyed peering through telescopes and daydreaming of imaginary spacecraft. Early on he kept his ambition of being an astronaut a secret, perhaps fearing that his dream was too big. But success in school and support from friends and family gave him confidence to reach for his goal.

Ellison received his college and graduate school education in aerospace engineering at the University of Colorado. He then entered the air force, becoming a flight test engineer. At age 32 he was selected from 8,000 applicants to become an astronaut. After becoming one, he took every chance to encourage young people to follow their dreams, often speaking at high schools.

Ellison was a mission specialist on the *Discovery* orbiter, becoming the first Hawaii-born, the first Japanese American, and the first Buddhist astronaut in space. In 1986 he and his crewmates on the space shuttle *Challenger* were killed in an accident that occurred at takeoff.

"Your education and imagination will carry you to places [that] we won't believe possible. Make your life count—and the world will be a better place because you tried."

ELLISON SHOJI ONIZUKA (1946–1986)

F is for Frank, architect with a bold, natural vision. When Frank Lloyd Wright was nine, his mother gave him a set of multi-colored blocks to encourage him to become an architect. Growing up in the Midwest, he loved the prairie and brought his love of nature into his designs.

Frank studied engineering for a year, but then—with only a few dollars in his pocket—he left for Chicago and found a job as a draftsman. Unlike many architects of his time, Frank believed American buildings should be different from European buildings. He soon joined a firm that promoted the idea that buildings should blend in with nature.

Frank designed buildings free of clutter, using the colors and forms of natural objects, such as waterfalls, honeycombs, and trees. He worked as an architect for 72 years, designing buildings all over the United States and the world, holding firm to his ideas even when others disagreed with him.

"We must study nature. Nature can show us how the principles of form and design are the inner rhythm of all beings. A genius is a man who has an eye to see nature, a man with a heart to feel nature, and a man with the boldness to follow nature."

FRANK LLOYD WRIGHT (1867–1959)

G is for Greg,

Olympic diver. Greg Louganis was born in San Diego to parents of Swedish and Samoan ancestry. Unable to care for him, his teenage parents gave him up for adoption. He excelled in gymnastics and acrobatics, but pursued diving after being encouraged by a coach. Despite his achievements in diving, Greg's childhood was sometimes difficult; he was teased for his skin color, his interest in dance, and his dyslexia, which was not diagnosed until much later. As a teenager he suffered from depression.

Coached by former Olympian Sammy Lee, Greg took the silver medal in platform diving at the 1976 Olympics. At age 22 he won the springboard and platform titles at the World Championships. Known for his grace as well as his strength and technical skills, he won the gold medal in both springboard and platform diving at the 1984 Olympics. He repeated this gold-medal performance in the 1988 Olympics despite testing positive for HIV.

Now an author and actor, Greg regularly appears at gay pride events.

"Fear is a part of everything you do. . . . You have to take great risks to get big rewards."

GREG LOUGANIS (1960–)

H is for Hiram, U.S. senator
and business leader. Born in Honolulu, Hiram Leong Fong was the seventh of 11 children in a Chinese immigrant family. He helped support his family even as a child. At age four he picked beans, and at age seven he shined shoes and sold papers. He attended the University of Hawaii and then went to Harvard Law School, leaving school twice so he could earn enough money to continue his studies.

After returning to Hawaii, Hiram started one of the first multi-racial law firms in the state and served as deputy attorney for Honolulu. He was elected to the territorial legislature and then to the U.S. Senate when the territory of Hawaii became the 50th state in 1959. He was the first Asian American to be voted to the Senate. As a senator he supported civil rights for people of all races and worked hard to improve educational opportunities for the people of Hawaii. After retiring from the Senate, Hiram continued running his businesses and opened a plantation and garden that was dedicated to preserving native wildlife and other plants.

"Be always positive and follow the truth."
HIRAM LEONG FONG (1906–2004)

Coconut Palm

Bamboo

Gardenia

Hibiscus

11

I is for Ivan, scientist and doctor.

Ivan Petrovich Pavlov was the son of a poor parish priest in Russia. As a child he hurt himself in a fall, which delayed his going to school. He entered the second grade of a church school when he was 11 years old. He might have become a priest, but after reading books by Charles Darwin, he decided to study chemistry and physiology.

At age 20 Ivan was admitted to the University of St. Petersburg. There he studied animal biology and learned how to conduct scientific research. He published works on blood circulation and digestion.

Ivan is best known for his experiments that showed how dogs salivate at the sight, odor, or footsteps of the person who feeds them. From these tests, he created the term *conditioned reflex* to show that dogs (and humans) respond to the activity associated with feeding, not just the feeding itself. Ivan's work paved the way for the scientific analysis of behavior. For his work on conditioned reflex, Ivan won the Nobel Prize in Physiology or Medicine in 1904.

"While you are experimenting, do not remain content with the surface of things. Don't become a mere recorder of facts, but try to penetrate the mystery of their origin."

IVAN PETROVICH PAVLOV (1849–1936)

J is for Jacques,

ocean explorer and environmentalist. As a boy Jacques-Yves Cousteau enjoyed making things, so he built a model crane and a battery-operated car. He was close to graduating from flight school when he had a serious car accident. To speed his recovery he began swimming, and soon after joined the French navy. In the navy he and a friend experimented with underwater breathing devices and invented scuba equipment.

Jacques converted a minesweeper-turned-ferry into a research vessel named *Calypso* and conducted many research trips. He wrote about encountering giant octopuses and hunting for sunken treasures. Sponsored by the French government, Jacques created a documentary on his adventures, including his experiment of living completely underwater for two months. In 1974 he founded the Cousteau Society, a non-profit organization dedicated to the study and preservation of the Earth.

"The future of civilization depends on water."
JACQUES-YVES COUSTEAU (1910–1997)

13

K is for Kahlil, artist and

writer. Kahlil Gibran was born and grew up in a small Lebanese village. Although he did not attend school, he listened to the stories of his neighbors, learning a great deal about the spiritual traditions of the Muslims, Druze, and Christians.

When Kahlil was 11, his mother moved the family to the United States to seek a better life. Impressed with his work, his art teacher introduced him to a photographer who became his mentor in literature and the arts. Kahlil sketched and painted portraits and book illustrations and then left the States to study literature at a college in Beirut.

Returning to the United States, Kahlil exhibited his art in Boston. With the help of patrons, he went to Paris to study painting. Soon after, he published essays and poems in Arabic and then later in English, including the best-selling book of parables titled *The Prophet*. Translated into many languages, *The Prophet* has inspired readers worldwide.

"Trust in dreams, for in them is hidden the gate to eternity."

KAHLIL GIBRAN (1883–1931)

14

L is for Langston, poet of the jazz-hot blues. When Langston Hughes was a baby, his father abandoned his mother. His mother raised him by herself until he moved to his grandmother's home.

In school Langston was surprised when his classmates elected him class poet as he had yet to write a poem. He eventually wrote one for his eighth-grade graduation. He also wrote poetry in high school, where he was a popular student. After graduating, Langston visited his father and convinced him to help pay for college. Although his father was against Langston becoming a writer, he agreed to help pay for college after Langston's poetry appeared in magazines.

In 1925 one of Langston's poems won first prize in poetry in *Opportunity* magazine and launched his writing career. He wrote many volumes of poetry, novels, and plays. A leading artist of the Harlem Renaissance, he was called the "Poet Laureate of the Negro Race." His original free verse gave a voice to the joys and bleakness of black American life.

"You have to learn to be yourself, natural and undeceived as to who you are, calmly and surely you."

LANGSTON HUGHES (1902–1967)

M is for Mohandas,

father of modern India. Mohandas Karamchand Gandhi was so shy as a boy that when school ended, he would run home so he would not have to talk to anyone.

At age 17 Mohandas left British-ruled India to study law in England. He later moved to South Africa to work. There he was shocked when he was rudely thrown off a train—even though he had a first-class ticket—because of his skin color. Mohandas then decided to lead a peaceful protest against the unfair laws of South Africa. After 21 years there, Mohandas, now called Mahatma, meaning "great soul," returned to India.

In 1919, after British soldiers opened fire on a group of protesters, Mahatma urged Indians to oust the British without violence. To help India become independent from England, he organized protests against unfair laws, often enduring long jail terms and harsh conditions as a result. He encouraged the Indian people to show their independence from British trade and rule by growing their own food and making their own cloth, salt, and other necessities. In 1947 Britain withdrew peacefully from India.

"An eye for an eye only makes the whole world blind."

MOHANDAS KARAMCHAND GANDHI (1869–1948)

N is for Nelson,

South African statesman. When Nelson Rolihlahla Mandela was a baby, his father was removed as a tribal leader because he stood up to an English judge over a dispute. The family had to move, but Nelson always remembered what his father taught him—to stand firm for what is right and fair.

As a young man Nelson moved to Johannesburg, where he worked and attended school. He joined the African National Congress (ANC), a group dedicated to abolishing apartheid, the system where nonwhites were forced to live, eat, and work in separate, inferior places.

As leader of the ANC, Nelson organized protests against apartheid. One night he was arrested and imprisoned under harsh conditions. Offered his freedom if he would renounce his work to abolish apartheid, Nelson stood firm for what he believed was right. When apartheid ended 27 years later, Nelson was freed and became the first elected president of the new South Africa.

"Education is the most powerful weapon [that] you can use to change the world."

NELSON ROLIHLAHLA MANDELA (1918–)

O is for Octavio,

Mexican diplomat and Nobel Prize–winning poet. The son of a journalist, Octavio Paz grew up in an old house with a jungle-like garden and what he called an "enchanted" room of books. He attended French and English schools and then studied law at the National Preparatory School. He left law school to start a school for workers.

In addition to writing poetry, Octavio did many things. He traveled to Spain to attend the Second International Congress of Anti-fascist Writers. He researched and published many nonfiction books and founded the literary journal *Taller*. He taught at several colleges and studied Asian literature and culture.

In 1945 Octavio joined the Mexican diplomatic service. He became the ambassador first to Japan and then to India, but he resigned from his post in India to protest the killing of student demonstrators in Mexico. During his life he published 30 volumes of poetry in Spanish, and his inspirational verse won the Nobel Prize for Literature in 1990.

"Poetry is knowledge, salvation, power, abandonment. An operation capable of changing the world, poetic activity is revolutionary by nature; a spiritual exercise, it is a means of interior liberation."

OCTAVIO PAZ (1914–1998)

P is for Pelé, soccer superstar.

Edson Arantes do Nascimento, known by his nickname, Pelé, was born in a small town in Brazil. Son of a soccer player, Pelé learned from his father how to kick a ball soon after he learned to walk. When he was 11, a retired soccer player helped him prepare for a professional career. Pelé tried out three times before he made the team at age 15, but he soon impressed the crowd with his strategy and accuracy.

At age 17 Pelé played soccer for the national Brazilian team, leading it to its first World Cup championship. With Pelé playing, the team won the World Cup in 1962 and in 1970. After retiring from soccer in Brazil, Pelé helped popularize soccer in the United States by playing for the New York Cosmos. In 1978 Pelé was awarded the International Peace Award for his work for children's causes through UNICEF.

"Enthusiasm is everything. It must be taut and vibrating like a guitar string."
PELÉ (EDSON ARANTES DO NASCIMENTO) (1940–)

Q is for Quincy,

musician, composer, and producer. Born in Chicago, Quincy Delight Jones Jr. had a tough childhood. Because of the mental illness of Quincy's mother, his father sent him and his brother to live with their grandmother. Quincy's grandmother was a former slave who saved money by having her grandsons catch rats, which she fried for dinner.

His father later returned for them, and they lived with a new stepmother and her children. Soon Quincy began studying music, learning piano, trumpet, trombone, and drums. At 14 he played in a small band with Ray Charles, often playing at clubs until early in the morning.

In addition to being a musician, Quincy wrote and arranged music for Frank Sinatra, Sarah Vaughan, Dinah Washington, Count Basie, and others. Today he writes music for movies and television. He produced the best-selling album of all time, Michael Jackson's *Thriller*, and the single, "We Are the World," which made $60 million to feed the hungry in Africa.

"The thing is to find your lightning—and ride your lightning."

QUINCY DELIGHT JONES JR. (1933–)

R is for Rudolf, the ballet

dancer who flew. When Rudolf Hametovich Nureyev was around six years old, his mother took him to the ballet. Captivated by the music and dancing, he decided then to become a dancer. He learned folk dancing and studied ballet, but his father later forbade him to study dance because he wanted him to be an engineer or doctor. But Rudolf still snuck out to take lessons.

By age 17 Rudolf had saved enough money to travel to an audition for the Leningrad Ballet School. He was accepted and worked hard to excel, even when it forced him to break rules, like leaving school to see performances. Upon graduation he joined the Kirov Ballet.

In 1961 Rudolf traveled with his ballet company to Paris and dazzled audiences. However, by this time he had had many conflicts with Russian authorities for disobeying the rules of his country. Rudolf longed for the freedoms the West had to offer. Convinced that he would soon be severely punished for his actions, he defected to the West. From there his career soared as he danced with companies all over the world, invigorating his ballets with his personal vision.

"In all my life, there has just been one love—dancing. I couldn't live without dance. When you watch me dance, you see [the] real me."

RUDOLF HAMETOVICH NUREYEV (1938–1993)

S is for Steven, legendary

filmmaker. At age 13 Steven Spielberg made his first movie, *Escape to Nowhere*, for which he won a prize. Known as a "weird, skinny" kid to his classmates, he won over the local bully by asking him to star in a movie he made using his father's camera.

During college Steven gained entrance to the back lot of Universal Studios and pretended to be an employee by dressing in a suit and carrying a briefcase. He successfully entered the studio and started talking with movie directors. His first commercial film, *Amblin*, impressed the studio executives so much that Steven dropped out of college to direct films and television shows. His movies include blockbusters like *Jaws, Raiders of the Lost Ark,* and *E.T.: The Extra Terrestrial*. Steven has also directed dramas like *Schindler's List*, a story of the Jews killed during the Holocaust. He used the profits from the film to start a foundation that videotapes the stories of Holocaust survivors.

*"I don't dream that much at night because
I dream all day. I dream for a living."*

STEVEN SPIELBERG (1946–)

T is for Tiger, master golfer.

Eldrick "Tiger" Woods got an early start in golf. He received his first golf club from his father when he was a baby, and he watched from his high chair as his father hit golf balls in the garage. At age four he won his first amateur golf tournament.

With the help of professional trainers, Tiger learned how to play confidently, even under difficult and pressure-filled conditions. He has had many victories, including being the youngest U.S. Junior Amateur champion at age 15, winning the National Collegiate Athletic Association (NCAA) individual title as a college student at Stanford University, and becoming the 1996 Professional Golfing Association (PGA) Rookie of the Year. Because of his achievements, Tiger has earned millions from tournaments and from athletic product endorsements. He also started a foundation to help disadvantaged children through golf and nonsporting activities.

"I don't just want to be the best black player ever . . . I want to be the best golfer ever."

TIGER (ELDRICK) WOODS (1975–)

U is for U Thant

(pronounced OO thant), international leader. Born under the name Maung Thant in Burma (now called Myanmar), U Thant was the oldest of four sons in a family dedicated to public service. He was an aspiring journalist and published his first article at age 16 in a magazine of the Burma Boy Scouts. After college graduation, he started teaching to help support his family.

Later known as U Thant, meaning "Uncle Thant," he became headmaster of his high school and published a book on the League of Nations, a precursor to the United Nations (UN). His friend was a leader in the Burmese nationalist movement, so U Thant joined as head of its publicity, later becoming the country's Minister of Information. At age 48 he was appointed Burma's representative to the UN and was later named UN secretary-general, the first non-European to hold the post. As secretary-general, U Thant worked hard to bring peace to the Middle East and to Vietnam. He also launched the first Earth Summit, established the UN Population Fund, and laid the foundations of the United Nations University.

"I feel more strongly than ever the worth of the individual human being is the most unique and precious of all our assets and must be the beginning and the end of all our efforts. Governments, systems, ideologies, and institutions come and go, but humanity remains."

U THANT (1909–1974)

V is for Vine, Native American

activist. Vine Deloria Jr. was born on a reservation in South Dakota. His great-grandfather was a medicine man, and his father was the first Native American to be a national executive of the Episcopal Church. When Vine was in the third grade, he got polio, which paralyzed his right leg. Vine dragged his leg on the ground when he walked. One day he climbed a steep hill. As he descended, he lost his balance. To stay upright he ran and his right leg began to move again. He was no longer paralyzed.

A Yankton Sioux, Vine attended schools on the reservation and in Connecticut. He graduated from Iowa State University and then studied at the Lutheran School of Theology. From 1964 to 1967 he was executive director of the National Congress of American Indians, learning much about politics, funding, and working with the U.S. government.

Vine felt he could do more to help the cause of Native American self-government by earning a law degree, so he went to the University of Colorado Law School. Throughout his career he has educated Native Americans about their rights through his teachings and writings. He has taught at many universities and written several books on Native American self-government, tribal society and spirituality, and the environment.

"When asked by an anthropologist what the Indians called America before the white man came, an Indian said simply, 'Ours.'"

VINE DELORIA JR. (1933–)

25

W is for Walt,
builder of dreams. When Walter Elias Disney was young, he dreamed of being a cartoonist, so he painted animals on the family's farmhouse and was punished by his father for it. Walt still loved art, and at age 20 he got his first job making short cartoons. He and a friend later started a company to make longer cartoons. When the business failed he moved to Hollywood.

With the help of his brother, Walt started the Walt Disney Studio, introducing *Mickey Mouse*, the first cartoon with synchronized sound. In 1932 he made the first full-color cartoon, and in 1937 he made the first full-length animated film.

Walt made many animated and live-action films, winning more than 30 Academy Awards. But he had another dream—to build an amusement park for families. He earned the money to build his park by producing television shows. Although some people made fun of his idea, in 1955 he opened Disneyland in California to instant acclaim.

"I think it's important to have a good hard failure when you're young."

WALT ELIAS DISNEY (1901–1966)

X is for Xavier, bandleader and king of the rumba. Francisco Xavier Cugat Mingall, called "X" by his friends, was born in Spain but grew up in Cuba. When he was five he received a quarter-size violin. Just months later Xavier was performing violin pieces in the neighborhood candy store.

Xavier studied music and as a young man debuted at Carnegie Hall as a violinist. Disappointed by poor reviews, he left for Los Angeles, where he met the actor Charlie Chaplin. Xavier played violin solos for Chaplin's movie soundtracks and later formed a Latin dance orchestra. Specializing in rumba, tango, and conga music, his band became a hit and was recruited to play at the Waldorf-Astoria Hotel in New York.

Xavier played at the hotel for 16 years and was featured on national radio shows. He also appeared in movies and launched the career of other musicians such as Desi Arnaz.

"I would rather play 'Chiquita Banana' and have my swimming pool than play Bach and starve."

Francisco Xavier Cugat Mingall

(1900–1990)

27

Y is for Yo-Yo, cellist and musical

ambassador. When Yo-Yo Ma was four, he learned cello from his father. Yo-Yo was so inspired by Bach, he learned the very difficult Bach Suites for cello two measures at a time. Yo-Yo studied music at the Julliard School in New York and attended Harvard University. In 1978 he won the Avery Fisher Prize, an award given to the world's best musicians.

Touring all over the world, Yo-Yo plays solos, chamber music, and orchestral music. He has recorded 50 albums, won 14 Grammy Awards, and contributed to many movie soundtracks. Yo-Yo seeks out new ways to share his music. He has appeared on *Sesame Street*, made two country-style albums with a fiddler and bassist, and created a video in which he teams up with a gardener, a choreographer, and two ice-dancing champions. He and jazz singer Bobby McFerrin recorded a CD titled *Hush*, which sold over a million copies. In 2001 Yo-Yo founded the Silk Road Project, which aims to connect the musical cultures of the United States, Europe, and Asia.

"Every time I open a newspaper, I am reminded that we live in a world where we can no longer afford not to know our neighbors. The Silk Road Project is a musical way to get to know your neighbors."

YO-YO MA (1955–)

Z is for Zoltán, composer and

music teacher. Born in a small town in Hungary, Zoltán Kodály spent much of his childhood in the countryside, where he learned about folk music traditions. His father, an amateur musician, encouraged his love of music. By the time he was in high school, Zoltán was composing his own songs.

Zoltán studied at the Franz Liszt Academy and the University of Hungary. He and his classmate Béla Bartók collected 3,000 folk songs by traveling through the countryside and recording them on a phonograph.

A teacher and then the director of the Budapest Conservatory, Zoltán composed works to be sung, works for instruments, and folk operas. He felt that it was important to bring music to the people and believed every child, rich or poor, should learn music. He developed a way of teaching music to children based on syllables (do, re, mi) and hand gestures. His approach, the Kodály method, has been taught around the world.

"Music is not a recreation for the elite, but a source of spiritual strength [that] all cultured people should endeavor to turn into public property."

ZOLTÁN KODÁLY (1882–1967)

29

Selected Bibliography
(alphabetical according to subject)

Kurosawa, Akira. *Something Like an Autobiography*. New York, NY: Alfred A. Knopf, 1982.

Richie, Donald. *The Films of Akira Kurosawa*. Berkeley, CA: University of California Press, 1996.

Easwaran, Eknath. *Nonviolent Soldier of Islam: Badshah Khan, a Man to Match His Mountains*. 2nd ed. Tomales, CA: Nilgiri Press, 1999.

Altman, Linda Jacobs. *Cesar Chavez*. San Diego, CA: Lucent Books, 1996.

Krull, Kathleen. *Harvesting Hope: The Story of Cesar Chavez*. San Diego, CA: Harcourt, 2003.

Winter, Jonah. *Diego*. New York, NY: Knopf, 1991.

NASA. Biographical Data, Ellison S. Onizuka (Lieutenant Colonel, USAF). http://www.jsc.nasa.gov/Bios/htmlbios/onizuka.html

Davis, Frances R. A. *Frank Lloyd Wright: Maverick Architect*. Minneapolis, MN: Lerner Publications, 1996.

The Official Greg Louganis Web Site. http://www.louganis.com

Asian American Portraits. New York, NY: Macmillan Library Reference, 2001.

Todes, Daniel Phillip. *Ivan Pavlov: Exploring the Animal Machine*. Oxford: Oxford University Press, 2000.

King, Roger. *Jacques Cousteau and the Undersea World*. Philadelphia, PA: Chelsea House Publishers, 2001.

Young, Barbara. *This Man from Lebanon: A Study of Kahlil Gibran*. New York, NY: Knopf, 1945.

Meltzer, Milton. *Langston Hughes*. Brookfield, CT: Millbrook Press, 1997.

Easwaran, Eknath. *Gandhi, the Man*. 2nd ed. Petaluma, CA: Nilgiri Press, 1978.

Gandhi, Mahatma. *An Autobiography: The Story of My Experiments with Truth*. Translated by Mahadev Desai. Boston, MA: Beacon Press, 1993.

McDonough, Yona Zeldis. *Peaceful Protest: The Life of Nelson Mandela*. New York, NY: Walker and Company, 2002.

Octavio Paz. VHS. Directed by Lewis MacAdams and John Dorr. Los Angeles, CA: The Lannan Foundation, 1989.

Burchard, S. H. *Pelé.* New York, NY: Harcourt Brace Jovanovich, 1976.

Jones, Quincy. *Q: The Autobiography of Quincy Jones.* New York, NY: Doubleday, 2001.

Maybarduk, Linda. *The Dancer Who Flew: A Memoir of Rudolf Nureyev.* Toronto: Tundra Books, 1999.

Powers, Tom. *Steven Spielberg: Master Storyteller.* Minneapolis, MN: Lerner Publications, 1997.

Teague, Allison L. *Prince of the Fairway: The Tiger Woods Story.* Greensboro, NC: Avisson Press, 1997.

UN Secretary-General Office of the Spokesman. U Thant Institute. http://www.un.org/apps/sg/sgstats.asp?nid=680

Malinowski, Sharon, and Simon Glickman, eds. *Native North American Biography.* New York, NY: UXL (an imprint of Gale Research), 1996.

Greene, Katherine, and Richard Greene. *The Man Behind the Magic: The Story of Walt Disney.* New York, NY: Viking, 1991.

Olde Time Cooking and Nostalgia. Xavier Cugat. http://www.oldetimecooking.com/music/xavier_cugat.htm

Yo-Yo Ma, Inspired by Bach. Falling Down Stairs. VHS. Yo-Yo Ma with Mark Morris. Directed by Barbara Willis Sweete. Produced by Rhombus Media. New York, NY: Sony Classical, 1995.

Blum, David. *Quintet: Five Journeys Toward Musical Fulfillment.* Ithaca, NY: Cornell University Press, 1999.

The Kodály Music Foundation Institute of Australia. The Person and Work of Zoltán Kodály. http://www.kodaly.org.au/

Author's Note

When my husband asked me to write a book on men similar to *Amelia to Zora*, I hesitated. I wondered if writing such a book would be as natural as writing about women. I also asked myself whether the world needed another book about men.

But then I began thinking of the men in my life who made a difference and the other men in the world who have helped all of us in such profound ways. As I did my research, I found it was a joy to celebrate men from many different fields, including the arts, exploration, and science.

I wanted to highlight a diverse group of contemporary men beyond celebrities, wealthy businessmen, and powerful heads of state. I particularly sought peacemakers because I believe these are the individuals who really change the world. Thus, it was important to me to include Mohandas Gandhi, Nelson Mandela, Cesar Chavez, and Badshah Khan.

No doubt you will be familiar with some of these men, but others you might not know. Each of them has many fascinating stories—stories of suffering, of struggle, and of hope.

I chose given names, rather than family names for each man so that "C is for Cesar" instead of "C is for Chavez." This is the same naming convention I used in *Amelia to Zora*. However, for two men, I fudged a little. Badshah Khan's given name is Abdul, but he was better known by Badshah (a title meaning "king"). The U in U Thant means "uncle," an honorary title in Burmese, but U Thant's given name is Maung.

Getting to know these men, I've learned a lot about living a life true to one's values. As you read their stories, I hope you will find the courage to change the world as they have.

Acknowledgments

The author thanks Randi Rivers, Donna Spurlock, Peter and Joshua Ching, Vanessa Pan, Nancy and William Chin-Lee, Carole and Steve Eittreim, Debbie Duncan, Debbie Keller, SuAnn and Kevin Kiser, Nancy Farmer, Heidi Kling-Reicherter, Kirk Glaser, and Nina Ollikainen.